MW01681135

HIS EYES

A journey with Jesus
Through His Passion—
Seen through His eyes

As revealed to
His humble handmaiden,
Anna

Illustrations by Regina-Champagne Babin

INFINITY PUBLISHING

All rights reserved. No part of this book shall be reproduced or transmitted in any form or by any means, electronic, mechanical, magnetic, photographic including photocopying, recording or by any information storage and retrieval system, without prior written permission of the publisher. No patent liability is assumed with respect to the use of the information contained herein. Although every precaution has been taken in the preparation of this book, the publisher and author assume no responsibility for errors or omissions. Neither is any liability assumed for damages resulting from the use of the information contained herein.

November 28, 2012
Nihil Obstat: Rev. Mitch Semar
Imprimatur: + Most Rev. Sam G. Jacobs
The nihl obstat and imprimatur are declarations that a book or pamphlet is free of doctrinal or moral error. No implication is contained therein that those who have granted the nihil obstat or imprimatur agree with the contents, opinions or statements expressed.

Copyright © 2011 by Priscilla Freeman and Regina-Champagne Babin
All art work, including the front and back covers were created by the artist: Regina-Champagne Babin

ISBN 978-0-7414-6776-9
Library of Congress Control Number: 2011934223

Printed in the United States of America

Published July 2014

INFINITY PUBLISHING
1094 New DeHaven Street, Suite 100
West Conshohocken, PA 19428-2713
Toll-free (877) BUY BOOK
Local Phone (610) 941-9999
Fax (610) 941-9959
Info@buybooksontheweb.com
www.buybooksontheweb.com

DEDICATION

I dedicate this book
In heartfelt gratitude:

First to My Lord and Savior Jesus Christ
Who found me worthy

To my sister Kay who gave me Scripture
It inspired me
For we are not only sisters in the flesh
But also in the Spirit

To my late friend Bob who gave me "the book"
It was the catalyst into this ocean

To my intercessory prayer group
Your prayers strengthened me

And to all my spiritual directors
Over the years
You were the voice of God and
My guides on this journey of faith

FOREWORD

You are about to embark on a journey deeply spiritual; one that will take you into the depths of what Jesus must have experienced, indeed suffered, in the consummation of the Very Work which the Father sent Him to do and for which He so willingly came among us as one of us...to save His people from their sins and the terrible consequence of sin; to reestablish fallen humankind on the path of Salvation, a destiny irrevocably lost through sin.

I have known the author, Anna, for the past 10+ years and have been blessed to have journeyed with her as this work was coming to fruition. She is an intensely prayerful and insightful person who relates intimately with her Lord in the course of her daily life. I know that she wants nothing more than to be his faithful disciple proclaiming the Kingdom at every opportunity by every manner to which she is drawn by grace. These reflections have been recorded within the context of prayer and at the promptings of the Holy Spirit.

Read prayerfully; it will move your heart to better understand just what it was that the God-Man suffered out of pure love for His ungrateful human creature. It will move you to reflection and to prayer, even to contemplation. It will impact your own relationship with your Savior in ways beyond description.

I strongly recommend Through His Eyes for the sincere seeker who wishes to come ever closer to his/her Lord.

Father Jerry Villarrubia

Illustrator, Regina-Champagne Babin

An artist takes the empty space of life to bring forth a spiritual creation. As a result, life is recorded. In this day of modern technology, there are still artists who create with the same hearts as our Renaissance artists seeking skill, purity, and holiness in what we define using visual tools. We search to behold the LOVE of God in all we portray to share with mankind. These pages of illustrations were created with paint, stone, mosaics, stained glass design, clay, etc. and a heart seeking insight from our Heavenly Father. With inspiration intertwined to stimulate thought, revelation, and compassion they are shared.

Born in New Orleans, growing up in the St. Charles Parish, and now residing in Terrebonne Parish, my life has been full with family, teaching art, illustrating and music. As a young self taught artist, I was constantly inspired and supported by wonderful parents, grandparents, six brothers an older sister, and numerous, magnificent cousins. Thus, I continue sharing life, art and music. My first printed work was as a teenager (left-C.1974)) published by my sister in New Orleans to share with loved ones. Because my grandfather loved it -saying it looked just like his vision in heaven, I have never stopped creating. My most memorable unveiling was in Houston, Texas with a mother/child portrait at a ladies' international convention (center-C. 1989). I pray artists will continue to unite in illustrating the greatest life told. The music written is a love song inspired by His Eternal Love.

"Que notre bon seigneur vous bénisse tous les jours du monde.»

INTRODUCTION

LUKE 2:36-38

"There was also a prophetess, Anna, the daughter of Phanuel, of the tribe of Asher. She was advanced in years, having lived seven years with her husband after her marriage, and then as a widow until she was eighty-four. She never left the temple, but worshipped night and day with fasting and prayer. And coming forward at that very time, she gave thanks to God and spoke about the child to all who were awaiting the redemption of Jerusalem." *(New American Bible)*

This Anna of long ago spoke about the Christ child. My God-given-name as the author of this book is Anna. I am the Anna of this time and of this age and I have been called to speak about the Man, Jesus Christ, Son of the Living God. I am to be an "expounder" *(one who explains or interprets)* and my mission is to expound upon the Passion of my Lord.

When I first received the message from the Lord to write this book, I balked. "Who am I, Lord, to do such a thing?" ran through my thoughts. Then the Lord reminded me of this Scripture passage:

PHILIPPIANS 4:13

"I have the strength for everything through Him who empowers me." *New American Bible*

My sister gave me the following Scripture several years prior to the writing of this book. I did not understand its true meaning until the Lord directed me to write. Now I hope she will understand its significance as well.

HABAKKUK 2:1-3

"I will stand at my guard post,
And station myself upon the rampart,
And keep watch to see what he will say to me,
And what answer he will give to my complaint.
Then the Lord answered me and said:
Write down the vision
Clearly upon the tablets,
So that one can read it readily.
For the vision still has its time,
Presses on to fulfillment, and
Will not disappoint;
If it delays, wait for it,
It will surely come, it will not be late."

(New American Bible)

With these Words to guide me—I was compelled to write. This book is written _Through His Eyes_. Jesus brings you His thoughts through me. He asks you to share the experience of His Agony, His Passion and His Crucifixion in a way you never may have before. It will not be easy; but, this is the road that will lead you to the Narrow Gate.

My sins, your sins, all sins past, present and future nailed Him to that cross. It was ***love*** that kept Him there. He who was sinless took upon Himself all sin. He became the perfect unblemished sacrifice to the Father. No one else could atone for all our sins.

Come and journey with Jesus—
Through His Passion—
As seen _Through His Eyes_—
As revealed to me
His humble handmaiden
Anna

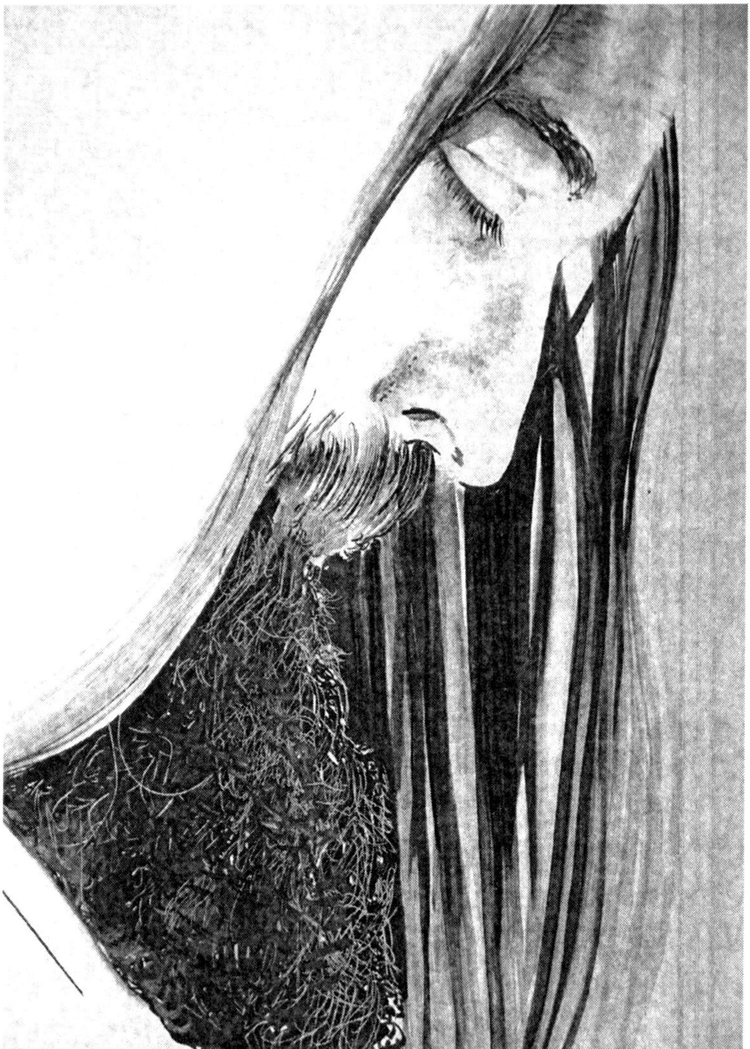

ABOUT THE AUTHOR
ANNA

My name is Priscilla Freeman. I reside in Houma, Louisiana—a city southwest of New Orleans. I am a senior citizen and a retired school teacher. I grew up on a sugar cane farm in the small town of Labadieville, Louisiana. My family lived with my maternal grandparents, who spoke only French, until I reached the age of 6. My heritage is diverse—Irish from my father and Cajun from my mother.

My parents and grandparents brought me up in the Roman Catholic Church—and my faith is very important to me. God is an integral part of my life. He is my "soul" provided and the source of all my strength.

God's call upon my heart to write this book began many years ago. It was a time of great pain and I found my solace in the Garden of Gethsemane in the arms of Jesus. He comforted me in my pain. It was here that He gave me His words.

COME

INVITATION
(from the Lord, Jesus)

Through My eyes
Journey with Me
As I take you
With Me
Down the road of
Agony
Condemnation
Degradation
Pain and
Death
But at the end
Of this road
Is life
Eternal salvation
Heaven
I rise from
The despair
Of death
I rise
Alive
Glorified
I defeat death
And I give you
That victory

Through My eyes
Journey with Me
See what I see
Come

MEDITATIONS

1. COME INTO THE GARDEN 1
2. ON MY KNEES 5
3. MY AGONY 9
4. THE QUESTION 13
5. SADNESS 17
6. THE TRIAL 21
7. SCOURGING 25
8. IMAGES 29
9. THE CROWN 33
10. VOICES 37
11. SAD, TIRED EYES 41
12. THE WEIGHT OF THE CROSS 45
13. VERONICA'S VEIL 49
14. I FALL 53
15. ON THE ROAD 59
16. 3 NAILS 65
17. COME TO THE FOOT OF THE CROSS 69
18. A MAN OF SORROW 73
19. HANGING HERE 79
20. BREATHE 83
21. TOUCH ME 87
22. SURRENDER 91
23. DEFEAT?—NO!!!—VICTORY!!! 95
24. WATER OF LIFE 99
25. COME INTO MY HEART 101
26. THE BLOOD OF THE LAMB 105
27. MY LOVE 109
28. FEELINGS 113
29. THE TORMENT 119
30. TOUCHES 125
31. I AM FORGIVENESS 131
32. UNION WITH ME 135
33. I GIVE ALL 139
34. HUMILITY 145
35. I CRY 149
36. AND THE FATHER CRIES 153
37. THE SORROWFUL MYSTERIES 157
38. SWEET BLOOD, BROKEN BODY 165
39. THE BATTLE 169
40. THE LIGHT 173

COME INTO THE GARDEN

Come into the garden
See Me here
I am cast down
Spent
Upon the ground
I am overwhelmed
In My grief

Come into the garden
See Me here
I am face down
Upon the earth
Begging My Father's ear
Distraught
And unabashed
My tears fall

I Am lamenting
For the sins
Against the Father
I Am crying out
For Him to take this
Cup from Me
And He is silent

Come into the garden
Touch My shoulder
Look into My eyes
The pain is Mine

You feel you are powerless
To help Me

Touch Me
Hold Me
I don't want to be alone

Come into the garden
How can I endure
What is to come

I bleed in My anguish

Oh! Look upon
My sorrow
Wipe away My tears
Break the deadly silence
Speak My name
As a caress

Come into the garden
Cry with Me for the
Iniquities committed
Pray to the Father with Me
And from Me
Learn to do His will

Come into the garden
I wait for you here

Reflections

Throughout this book, you will find "empty reflection" pages. As you meditate on the passages you have read, allow the Lord to guide your pen and to reveal His thoughts for you.

Anna

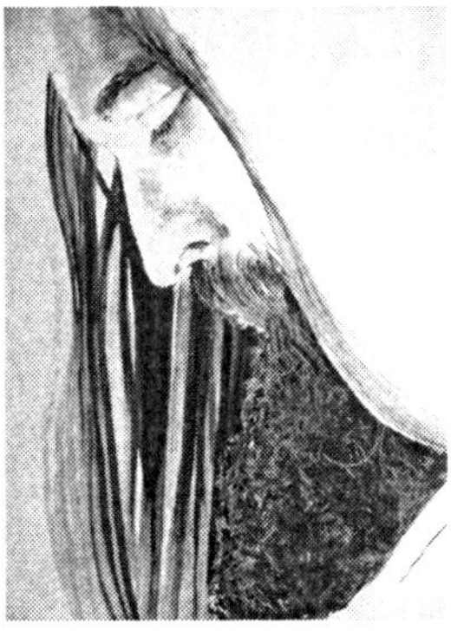

ON MY KNEES

The enormity of what
Is about to happen to Me
Overwhelms Me
The sins of mankind
Weigh Me down
My knees begin shaking
My stomach is in knots
I Am sweating profusely
And I Am afraid
A deep cold fear
Deep within Me
Builds

I cannot stand
I fall to My knees
And I cry out to My Father
And I cry
And I sweat blood
In My distress

And the Father is silent

My will wants
This cup
Taken from Me
And again I plead
With My Father

And again

Silence

He does not answer

It is not until
I surrender
My will to His
That I experience peace
A peace that replaces
My fear and gives Me the
Strength to fulfill My destiny

And My Father honors Me
Not with His words
But with an angel
To comfort Me

Learn from Me

On your knees
Shall you come to Me

Reflections

Agony
Despair
Clutching
I BLEED TEARS OF BLOOD
I SEE THE SINS OF MANKIND
LONLINESS
Pain
MY BODY MY PAIN MY BLOOD

MY AGONY

Agony
There are many who fear the word
Agony
There are many who understand it not
Agony
An experience in terror
An experience in peace
One word—different outlooks

My agony
I Am swimming in pain
With no sign of relief
Praying to drown
But knowing I won't
The uncertainty of the unknown
Sends Me into the
Depths of despair
Fear intermingles with pain
Screaming to be released

My agony
Falling to My knees
Before My Father
In the Garden of Tears and Blood
My Garden of Gethsemane

My agony
I see the sins of mankind
As they are placed upon Me

And I become sin

I Am the victim
And perfect sacrifice
In the sight of My Father

My agony
Deep
Indwelling darkness
Surrounding Me
Clutching at My every breath
My heart racing
As I dwell on the inevitable.

My agony
My humanity
Crying for release
And My spirit
Knowing there will be none
Until My work is done
Hanging on the cross
Giving My life for you
The aloneness closes in around Me
Like the dark clouds
Of an approaching storm
My friends are asleep

My agony
I know what is to come
And I cry
I tremble
I foresee My passion
The pain
The torture yet to come
And

I sweat drops of blood
I bleed
The first offerings
For the Father
One drop would suffice
Yet I give all
As it falls to the earth
And soaks the ground
Redemption is born

Not My will, Father
But Yours be done

I Am alone in the universe
An angel comes
From the Father
To bring Me comfort
A promise for you as well
In your hour of need
The birth of Hope

I come face to face with death
And I win
The victory is Mine
And therefore—yours
For all time and eternity

Agony
Fear it not
For I have glorified it
In My Blood

THE QUESTION

The torture of the mind
Can be far greater than
The torture of the Body
In agony
I pray
I know

My mind is plagued
With thoughts
My humanity screams out
For release
I pray to My Father
I know what is to come
This sorrowful night
I see the torture
The agony
The pain yet to come
And yet I ask the Father
This question
My Father, can this
Cup pass from Me

[Silence]

I know what I must do
Not My will, Father
Not My will
I pray
I know

I know what I must do

An understanding surfaces
I know
I love all creation
I know
This will save them

[Silence]

I pray
I know
I speak
This sacrifice will
Bring them to You, Father
I must surrender
I pray
I know
I speak
Your will, Father
Not Mine must be done
Your will, Father
Not Mine be done

I love You so much, Father
I offer Myself
Willingly to You, Father
For them
Take Me
I'm Yours
There is no other way
I pray
I know

[Silence]

Reflections

SADNESS

A deep sadness
It penetrates My being
It is borne from within
It pervades My being
It surrounds and engulfs Me

As wave upon wave of sins
Are laid upon Me from of old
Are laid upon Me from now
Are laid upon Me
From the future yet to come

A deep sadness
It penetrates My being
A weight upon My mind
Upon My soul
A weight upon My back
I cannot lift it
I Am dragged to the ground

The filth of generation
Upon generation of sin
Is poured upon Me
The abyss created
Between man and Creator
Must be crossed

I fall into the darkness beneath

And a deep sadness

Penetrates My being

Feel My anguish
I Am weary
I Am brought down
Yet I know in the
Depth of My soul that
I Am that bridge
Across the chasm

And the sadness of the Father
Penetrates My being

It seeps in
Deeper and deeper
And I bleed in agony
I struggle
In the depths of despair
I know no relief
Other than
To give My life for all

I must surrender all

I must die
In atonement for sins

And the sadness of the Father
Penetrates My being

FATHER
BEHOLD THE BRIDGE

Reflections

THE TRIAL

The trial is a farce
Liars are paid
To bear false witness
The prince of lies
Spreads his malice this night
And many
Believe the falsehoods

Men of honor speak lies
In fear of losing
Their position and power
Ambition is the ruler
Of my accusers' hearts

Pompous arrogance
Is displayed
Under the disguise
Of righteousness

I listen
I Am accused of blasphemy
I AM God's Son
The truth is overwhelming
They cannot bear it
And they condemn Me

Fainthearted
They bring Me to the
Roman authorities
They seek to pass the blame
But forever
My Blood will be
Upon their hands

I Am alone

My companions
Have deserted Me

Peter has denied Me

Alone I must walk down
This pathway of infamy

Alone I must bear this
Agony and pain

I walk in silence
Like the innocent Lamb
To the slaughter

My destiny is at hand
The fulfillment of the
Prophecies begins

Reflections

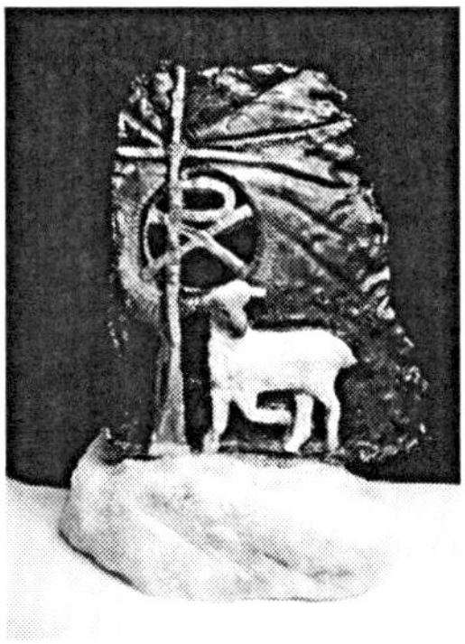

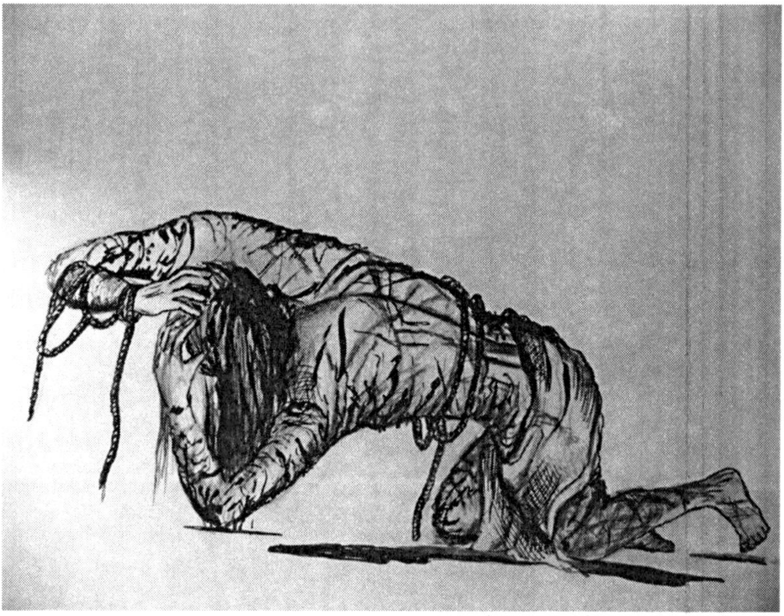

SCOURGING

They strip Me
And tie Me to a post
In the courtyard
They stand back
To watch and laugh

I call you
To stand behind the post
And look upon the whip master
Then look into My eyes
Journey with Me
Into this Sea of Pain

I hear the whip singing
And tongues of fire
Explode upon My back

My body is slammed against the post
And the whip recoils

It sings again
And My back is seared in pain
Whelps rosy and long begin to appear
Row
Upon row
Upon row

My skin is cut and lacerated
From the pieces of metal
Tied to the lash

The whip sings

Again
And again
And again

Drawing blood
Thick and oozing
Trickling to the ground

Tears fall from My eyes
To mingle with the blood
Rolling from My wounds
And down My legs

I Am standing
Barely
In a puddle of My own blood
It gathers round My feet
It soaks the ground
First in the Garden
And now—here

The whip sings
Again
And again
And again

I utter not one word
To silence
All the excuses of Adam
Before the Father

The ground is slippery

And I can no longer stand
I crumble to My knees
And the whip continues to sing

From somewhere
Ever so faintly
That command is spoken
Halt

And the whip is silent

My back is open
To so many wounds
That no skin remains

My clothes are thrust upon Me
I am so weak
I cannot stand

I am dragged
Before the Procurator
Who screams
Look at the Man

Yes,
Look upon Me
See My pain

See My love for you
And go
And sin no more

IMAGES

Picture this:
I sit in the Pretorium
Pushed and prodded

The scouring has left Me weak
I can hardly remain awake

The guards allow Me no rest
No sleep this cold dark night

The wounds that were
Caked in blood
Are opened
And bleed anew

The spittle of vile men
Runs down My face
To wet My garments

The smell of death is
Upon Me

I am an object of ridicule

They call Me King
And laugh
Soon I will reign in glory
But not this night

This night I must endure
The agony—
The sarcasm—
The pain

Pain of a magnitude you
Cannot comprehend

Pain beyond all human endurance

Pain beyond the physical

Pain of complete abandonment
And deep sorrow

Pain of sadness
Felt to the core of My being

Pain in My soul
For the sins of all mankind

Picture all this:

The pain of God

And know what it means
When I say I love you

REFLECTIONS

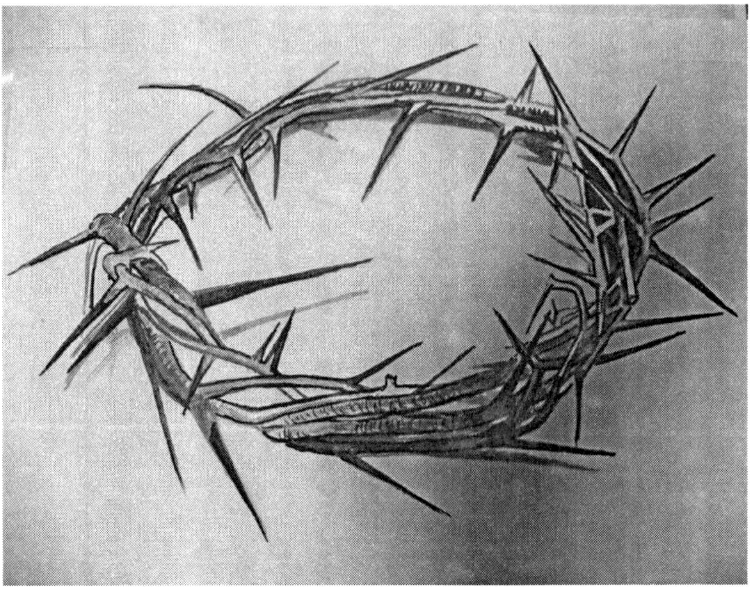

THE CROWN

Mocking tongues
Crown of pain

Piercing deeply
Drawing Blood
Face gaunt
Spittle dripping
Purple robe

Crown of pain
Mocking tongues

Thorns of hate
Driven deeply
By men of fury

Crown of pain
Mocking tongues

Hearts of fear
Understanding not
Feeling threatened

Crown of pain
Mocking tongues

Herod laughing

Soldiers hitting
Man of Sorrow

Crown of pain
Mocking tongues

Stone cold room
Stone cold hearts
Stone cold revile

Crown of pain
Mocking tongues

Exhausting night
Shivering body
Chattering teeth

Crown of pain
Mocking tongues

Plucking beard
Sweet Blood flowing
Sad eyes
Tired eyes

Crown of pain
Mocking tongues

Tears of pain

Tears of sorrow
Tears for the lost

Crown of pain
Mocking tongues

No rest is Mine
No blissful sleep
Constant torture

Crown of pain
Mocking tongues

Crown of pain
Not of glory
King of Kings
Speaking not

Silent Lamb
Before the shearers

Son of God
Wearing a
Crown of pain
Listening to
Mocking tongues

CRUCIFY HIM!
CRUCIFY
HIM
CRUCIFY
HIM
CRUCIFY
HIM!

VOICES

Condemnation
The Son of God
Is condemned by the masses

Crucify Him

Rings in My ears
Chills My soul
I Am bleeding and
My body is so cold

Crucify Him

Screamed by foes

Crucify Him

Screamed by those
Who were once
My followers

The sins
Committed by you
Scream too

Crucify Him

Crucify Him

How My heart aches
And sadness resides
Deep within
As these words
Are branded into
My troubled mind

Crucify Him

Rejection
Of a magnitude
I cannot explain

I Am the Son of God
Condemned
Abandoned
Alone

No words are spoken
To comfort Me

The only words
resounding
In My ears are

CRUCIFY HIM

Reflections

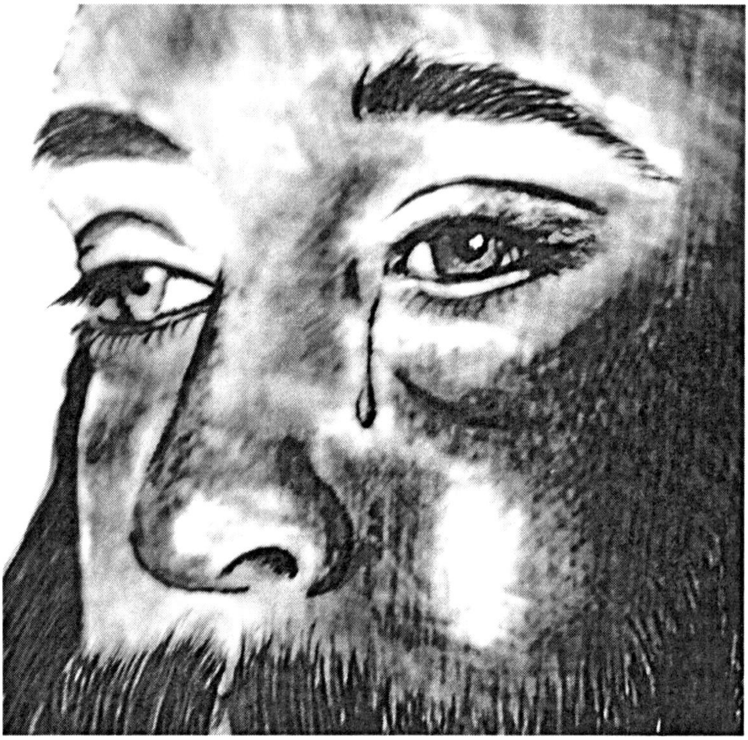

SAD, TIRED EYES

Sad, tired eyes
Look longingly
At the passers by

Sad, tired eyes
Search
For familiar faces and
Find only angry men

Sad, tired eyes
Cry
As blood trickles in
As followers are recognized
And turn away

Sad, tired eyes
Cry
As those once healed
Turn away

Sad, tired eyes
Shed tears
For the lost and forsaken
Who cannot see
For the found
Who choose not to see
And
For the agony yet to come

Sad, tired eyes

Close briefly
Softly
From exhaustion
As the wood cuts deeply
Into the flesh

Sad, tired eyes
Open wide
To feel the lash
Upon the back

Sad, tired eyes
Close briefly
As sandaled feet
Slowly
Slowly
Take another step

Hurry is the cry
Yet sad, tired eyes
See
The hill beyond
And the agony
And final pain
Yet to come

Then sad, tired eyes
Smile widely and
Shine brightly
With inner strength
For the Promise
Yet to come

Reflections

THE WEIGHT OF THE CROSS

The weight of the cross
Bears down on Me
I feel the burden of it
Into the depths of My soul

The weight of the cross
Bears down on Me
I must walk the path
Alone
With no one
To help Me
With no one
To stop the infamy
Yet to come

The weight of the cross
Bears down on Me
My chest constricts
As I fight to breathe

You can not bear
This burden
It is far beyond you
I Am the Chosen One
As I walk
And stumble My way
To My crucifixion

The weight of the cross
Bears down on Me
The sins of mankind
Are upon My shoulders

And it brings Me down
To My knees
Once
Twice
Three times
And three times
I rise

I leave a trail of blood
Drop by drop
My blood is shed
For you
From the Garden of Gethsemane
To the foot of the cross

Drop by drop
Soaking the earth
Appeasing the Father
Releasing the power
Of grace
Destroying Satan
Opening Heaven's gates

The weight of the cross
Bears *down* on Me
Until it bears Me *up* upon it
And I set you free

REFLECTIONS

VERONICA'S VEIL

I Am stumbling
Barely able to stand

I Am blinded by
The blood sweat and tears

The cross is heavy
Upon My back

And from the crowd
Proudly walks a woman

She defies all reasoning
And comes to Me

She gently wipes My face
With her veil

I am refreshed

The softness of her veil
Brushes gently on
My bloody face
Disfigured by
The beatings
The crown of thorns
The plucking of My beard

She has come to comfort Me

And for her boldness

For her courage

For her compassion

For her love

I give her a gift

My face imprinted
Upon her veil

And graces flood her soul

She is healed

She is forgiven

She is forever changed

Veronica, thank you

Reflections

I FALL

I Am on the Road
With the cross
Upon My back
I fall
My hands
Reach out
To brace My fall
And take the full impact
As My Body
Crumbles
My knees hit
The ground
The cross hits too
The force of My fall
Causes My head
To jerk backward
And to
Hit the cross
My head bursts into
Renewed pain with
Throbbing crescendos
And I bleed anew
The whip comes down
Upon Me
As though this added
Torture could
Possibly give Me
Strength enough to rise

I dig deep within
My being
And discover
A strength
I did not know I had
And slowly
Ever so slowly
I rise
My hands push
My upper body up
As I rest on My heels
I lean forward and
Push with My feet
I stand and
Lift the cross
And the relentless whip
Urges Me
To move faster
Once standing
I wait
My arms dangling
By My side
The weight of the cross
On My torn
Opened shoulder
Causes renewed suffering
I embrace the cross and
I begin walking
Blood is running down
My Body from head to toe
Sapping My strength
I Am dizzy
I Am light-headed

Nauseous
I Am starved
And dehydrated
And
I fall again
The second time is worse
The palms of My hands
Are now opened and bleeding
Covered with dirt
And the filth from
The ground
My knees are bruised
The force of the impacts
Has caused blood vessels
To open and bleed
Under My skin
The process of rising
Begins again
The whip—and
The anger of the soldier
Wielding it
Brings sadness to My heart
I pray for him
For all of them
I know what must be done
And again
I rise
Step by aching step
Onward I walk
Until
I fall again

This third time
I Am prostrate
Upon the ground
The force of this impact
Reverberates throughout
My broken and battered body
My head is jolted
As My jaws
Are slammed together
New bruises come forth
Immediately
My body is worn
My strength diminished
I cannot get up
This time

The soldiers
Grab roughly at Me
They bring Me to My feet
They will not be robbed
Of this execution
They push and shove
And I walk
Slowly
Painfully
To the Place of the Skull
Calvary
And My death

Reflections

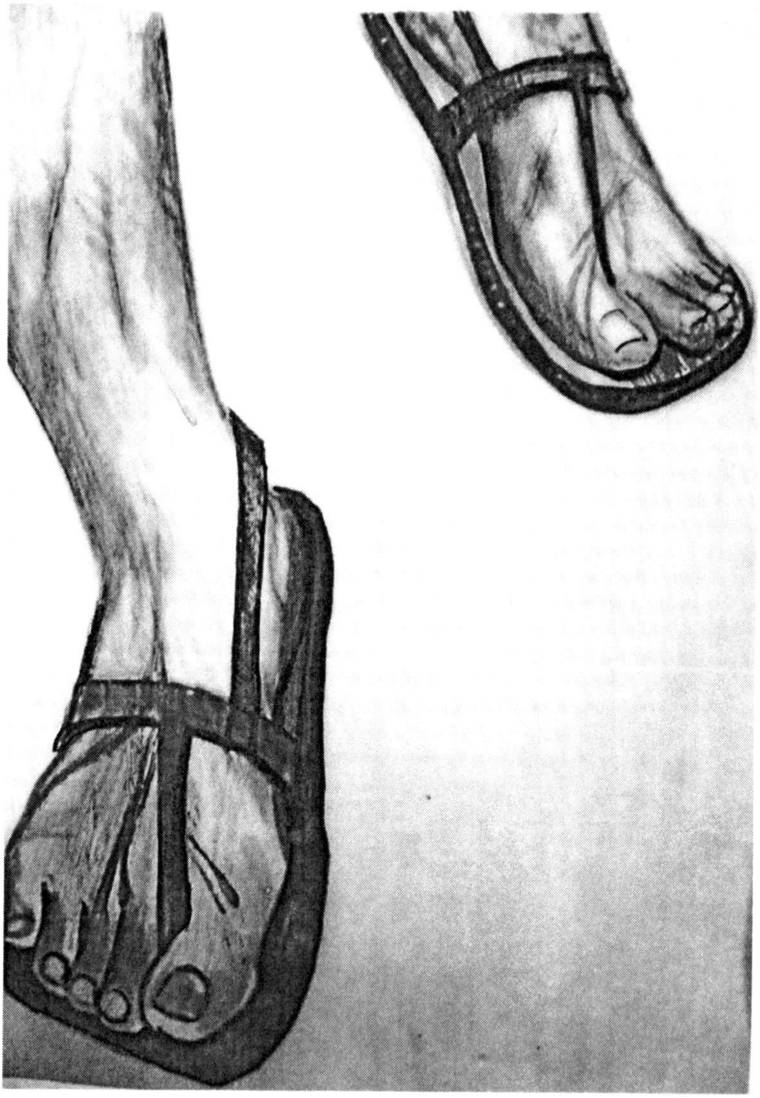

ON THE ROAD

On the road to death
I walk
Slowly
Bleeding
The scourging
Has sapped My strength
Onward I trod
Undulating pain reverberates
Throughout My body
With every step I take
Old wounds are opened and
New ones created
My head throbs
As the crown of mockery
Digs into My skull
Blood trickles down My face
To fall unobserved
Into the earth
Below My feet

On the road to death
I walk
Yet I know it is the
Road to Life
The Dolorosa for all
Can you walk with Me
Come
Stand beside Me
Walk step by step with Me

Look at Me
The Lamb
The cross bears down upon Me
It tears My flesh
And reaches bone
I cry in excruciating pain
I do not ask you
To carry My cross
Nor My burden—
The sins of the world
Carry instead My sadness
In your heart
Wipe away My tears
With your repentance
Dress My wounds
With your love

On the road to death
I walk
I fall
Where Oh Father is My strength
I must get up
I must move on

On the road to death
I walk
My head is downcast
I hear cursing
Where once were blessings
But if I listen carefully
My remnant cries for Me
Today

And
In all generations to follow
It comforts Me
Are you still here with Me
Do not abandon Me

On the road to death
I walk
I stumble
I fall
I cannot go on
Help Me
The cross is so heavy
I have not the strength to lift it
Your presence here with Me
Gives Me the courage to walk on
The agony of pain
Tears at My consciousness
But I have resolve
From where does it come
My Father
My love for Him
I AM the obedient Son
I get up

On the road to death
I walk
No—I Am not walking
I Am staggering
The cross is heavy
Upon My shoulders

Even Simon of Cyrene
Feels its weight
I am pushed and shoved
Where once
I was touched in awe
So sweetly
So reverently
What has happened
What has changed
My whole body throbs
With each heartbeat
With each ragged breath
With every step I take

On the road to death
I walk
I am dying
I fall
I feel the whip once more
I slowly lift My head
And see "The Hill"
Golgotha
The Place of the Skull
My destiny
I embrace it
I must reach it
It is all part of The Plan
Help Me up
It's time

Reflections

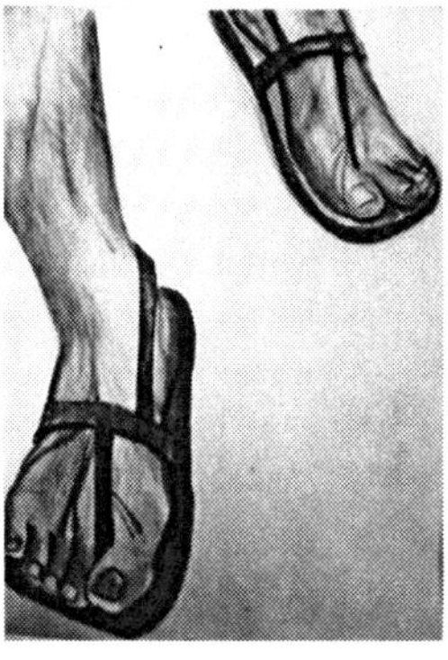

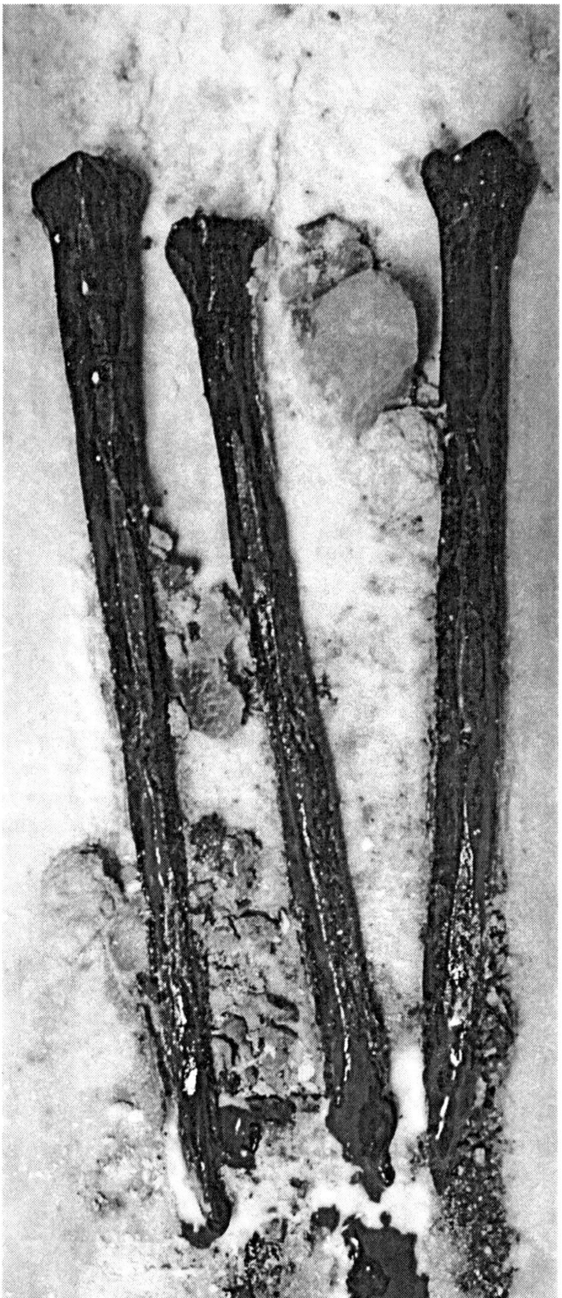

3 NAILS

I have reached The Hill
My clothes
Are ripped from My body

Taking skin and flesh
From wounds
Caked in dried blood
I bleed anew

3 NAILS
Cold hard iron

Tearing flesh

Shattering nerves

Uncontrollable spasms

Unrelenting pain

2 NAILS
Holy Hands

Callused hands

Carpenter's hands

Hands of mercy

Healing hands

Unrelenting pain

1 NAIL

Sandaled feet

Washed in tears

Walking roads

To crowds in need

Bleeding freely

Unrelenting pain

3 NAILS

Hammered deeply

Driven slowly

Tears of pain

Silent weeping

Indifference rampant

Unrelenting pain

Reflections

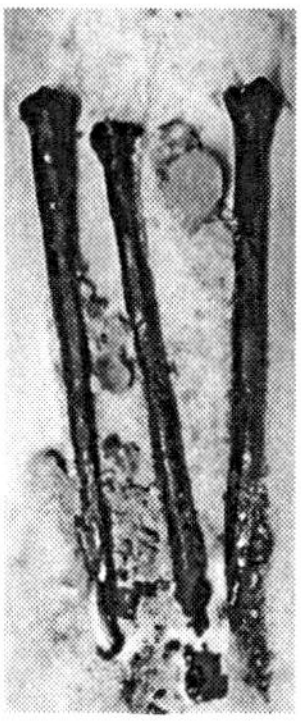

COME TO THE FOOT OF THE CROSS

Come to the foot of the cross
Here you will find healing
Here you will find strength
For the tasks ahead
For the road to travel
For the journey to Me

Come to the foot of the cross
Here you will find sadness
And sorrow and pain
And rising above it all
You will find Me
And joy

Come to the foot of the cross
Your cross is not easy to carry
But when you place it
Upon Mine
It is no longer burdensome

Come to the foot of the cross
Let My Blood fall upon you
Let it wash you clean
Let it run over you
And seal you

Come to the foot of the cross
Kiss My bloodied feet
Taste the bitterness
That I bear

Taste the sweetness
In dying for friends
Taste the pain that
Racks My body as it
Shudders uncontrollably

Come to the foot of the cross
Be the friend that
Does not abandon Me
Yearn to wipe the tears
From My eyes
Desire with all your heart
To cover My shame

Come to the foot of the cross
And cry for Me
And cry with Me
Don't turn away from
My disfigured and
Battered body
Soon it will be transfigured
And the Glory of God
Will shine
Through Me
With Me
In Me

Come
Oh! Come
To the foot of the cross

Reflections

A MAN OF SORROW

I Am a Man of Sorrow
Look upon Me
Look at what I do
For you
I come down
From Heaven

Time—
I who exist outside
Of time
I enter
Into time
I come
To walk among you

Sorrow—
I grieve
I take on your
Mortal flesh
Me
God
The Great I AM
Infinite
Majestic
Spirit
I become dust so that
You may have
Eternal life

Suffering—
I suffer great pain
Unbearable torture
My body riddled
With agony
I die for you
A horrific death
The death of a criminal

Endurance—
I endure
Ridicule
Abandonment
Sadness
Of a magnitude
You will never
Understand

I created you
And you turn
Against Me

You sin

And hurt Me

With a magnitude
You will never
Understand

Look upon—

This Man of Sorrow
Don't turn away
Look upon every
Bloody part
I Am covered
With bruises
And blood runs from
The multitude of wounds
Upon My
Dying body

Look upon—
This Man of Sorrow
Stop
Don't turn away
Don't just walk by
Look at Me
Upon My cross
Shed a tear
For Me

Time—
Truly
I call you to spend
Time with Me
More than a glance
More than a thought
Time spent
In meditation
On all
I give up for you

Know in your heart
I would do it
Over
And over
And
Over again
To save your soul
Even if you were
The only person
On earth

I live for you
I die for you
So great is
My love for you

Look upon—
This Man of Sorrow
And see the joy
Of a magnitude
You will never
Understand
When I greet one
Lost soul in Paradise

And some day

You

Reflections

HANGING HERE

I hang in sorrow

As pain electrifies
And erupts
Throughout My body
Causing spasms that ripple
Through Me
Creating new terror
And torture
As the weight of My body
Pulls against the nails

My spirit buckles
Under the weight
The burden of sins
Committed in the past
The present
And those yet to come

And still My spirit rejoices
That soon My Father
Will be appeased

And all mankind
Will be redeemed

My Blood
Falls freely

Shed willingly
For mankind
As I hang in sorrow
For your sins too

My chest heaves
And My lungs burn
With each
Ragged breath
I draw

To inhale I must
Pull Myself up
Against the cross
Iron pulls and tears flesh
I feel as though
My hands and feet are
Being ripped apart

Splinters imbed in
My wounded back
I exhale
And sag against the wood
Splinters imbed anew
Every breath brings
The same agony

For 3 hours
I draw breath

In and out

In and out

And
The Agony is renewed
Each time

I hang in sorrow

Inwardly I scream

Yet outwardly I Am silent

I bear this pain
Before the world
As it waits
And watches

Every fiber of My being
Cries out for an end
To the pain

And yet I wait

Obedient to the end

BREATHE

My skin crawls
With raw sensations
As just the breeze
Upon My body
Brings feelings of
Burning
Cold
And tears

I shiver
Unable to control the
Tremblings deep within
Rippling upward
To cause
Uncontrollable shaking

And fear
Fear of falling
Fear of dying
Fear of the unknown
My humanity cries out
For relief

Muscles ache beyond belief
I Am trying to hold Myself
Up on the cross

To sag is to bring
Untold agony

Yet sag I must for I
Have not the strength
To straighten up

Breathing
Is near impossible
The struggle
The process
Almost too much
To bear
I hold My breath
As long as I can
And then instinctively
I breathe

I must breathe
I straighten up
As best I can
And Inhale
My breath is cut short
As pain rips through Me
I exhale
Collapse
And sag once more
I beg and pray that
This breath will be
My last

But then the whole sordid
Process repeats itself
Over
And
Over again

As the seconds turn
To minutes
And the minutes
To hours

I want to let go
But I persevere
I endure
Until I release
My Spirit to the Father

I Am helpless
Alone
The Innocent Lamb
Slaughtered
For the sins of the nation
For the atonement
Of the sins of man

ALL FOR THE FATHER

TOUCH ME

Touch Me
What do you fear
Touch Me
What holds you back

As I walk by
Touch Me
With your hands
Gently let Me feel
Your presence
I need
To desperately
Feel the human touch
For I Am dejected
Dying
Walking to My death

Touch Me
What do you fear
Touch Me
What holds you back

As I hang
Touch Me
In misery and pain
I hang
Upon the cross

Put your hand
Upon My wounds
To stem the flow
Of blood
My life giving force
Softly
Sweetly
Flowing out
Unto the earth below

Touch Me
What do you fear
Touch Me
What holds you back

Touch My nerve-racked
Hands and feet
They are so sensitive
That the slightest touch
Would bring
Indescribable torture

But **your** touch
Will bring a brief
Requital

Touch Me

What do you fear
Touch Me
What holds you back

Touch your lips
To the wounds
Upon My broken body
Kiss them with
The softness of a lover
Touch Me with the dew
Of your tears
Let them fall upon
My pierced feet
To wash the dirt
And blood away

You are standing
Too far away
Come closer
You cannot touch Me
Unless you come nearer
To the seat of pain
To the fount of love
Some come only to look
You cannot feel Me
With your eyes

Don't be afraid
Come closer and
Touch Me

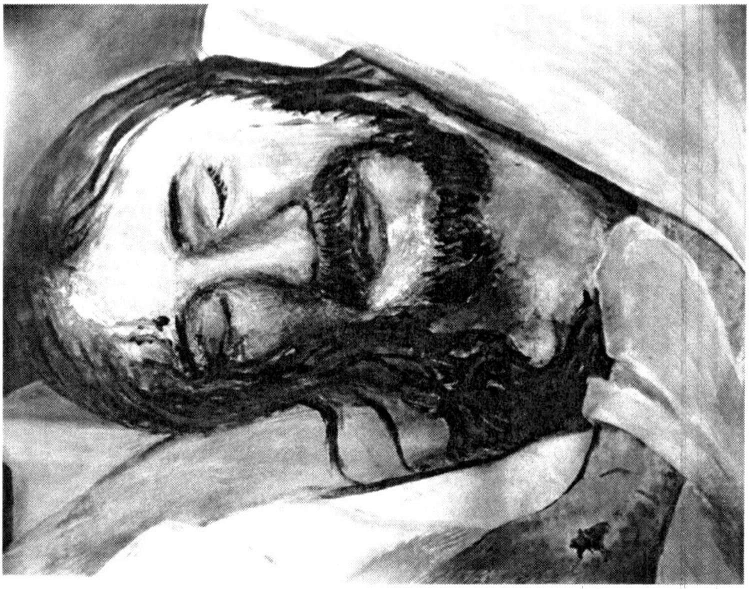

SURRENDER

There is an ache in
My chest
A constricting force
Of unknown origin
It seeks My demise
It seeks to take Me
From My path

I will not surrender
I will not give in

My mortal body
Cries out in intense pain
It screams to My mind
To let go
Yet I fear
This unknown path

I Am human like you
And I feel a panic
Rise up in Me
I do not want to
Release My body

This darkness around Me
I do not understand it
I fear what I
Cannot comprehend

My agony increases
I Am brought down
Bowed over in pain
It hurts so much

My skin crawls as
A gentle breeze caresses
My broken body
Even this
Brings Me pain

Release
Sweet release
I must go to My Father
But first—I must die
This incomprehensible thought
I must embrace it
My humanity cringes
At the idea
How

I speak
Father into Thy Hands I
Commend My Spirit
I must lead the Way
And so it is done
It is finished
I SURRENDER
I die
In the throes of pain

And My Spirit is set free
And I Rise

Reflections

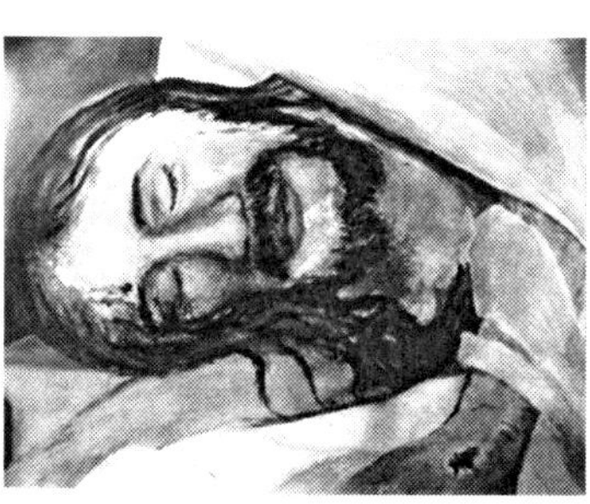

DEFEAT?—NO!!!—VICTORY!!!

The agony of defeat
This is what they see
This crowd of watchers
As I hang here
They see with the eyes of man
And not beyond

I Am broken and abused
And silent
I do not seek retaliation
Or retribution
And they do not understand
I Am an enigma
In their eyes

But the thrill of victory is Mine
Amidst the pain and the suffering
I see the end result
Glory unbounded
For those who come to Me
By way of the cross

The agony of defeat
A pitiful man
Condemned to a
Criminal's death
Look upon Me
With the eyes of faith
And see the Son of God
Redeemer of all mankind

Look beyond the brokenness
And the Blood
And see your Savior
Not the mighty warrior king
But the humble majesty
Of your Lord

The agony of defeat
Weighs heavy on the
Hearts of My disciples
Long ago and even now
In this day

To comprehend such love
Is beyond them
And perhaps beyond you
That I could give
My life willingly

This
For some men
Is a paradox

Never doubt
Believe in Me
For there is no defeat in Me
Only love of the Father
And obedience to His will
And victory
And joy
And above all these
LOVE

Reflections

WATER OF LIFE

I cry
And My tears are
Living water
Shed for you
A river of life
Where all can partake
Come
Drink your fill
Be refreshed
In the Water of Life

My side is opened
My heart is pierced
Blood and water
Pour forth
Here is the Fount
Of Life and Mercy

Come
I call you
Stand beneath the cross
Be washed clean
In the Water of Life

I cry
I die
For you
That you might be free
Come
To the Water of Life
Come

COME INTO MY HEART

Come into My heart
There's a cut in it
Where you can
Crawl in

My Blood
Is being shed
Falling to the earth
Darkening the dirt

It's a pool at My feet
Rich and red
Covering the filth
Enriching the poor

Come into My heart
There's a cut in it
Where you can
Crawl in

Let it encase you
Surround you
Give you peace
Fill you with
Its life-giving force
Takes you away from
This world with
All its worries

My heart is opened
By a lance
Driven in hate
Releasing love and mercy
Enough for all mankind
Until the end of time
Enough for you

Come into My heart
There's a cut in it
Where you can
Crawl in

Come into My heart
It's a sacred place
Shared with special friends
Come
You are My special friend

Come into My heart
It's breaking
From words and from deeds
But I offer it for all
A debt I must pay

Come into My heart
There's a cut in it
Where you can
Crawl in
Come in
And
Let Me love you

Reflections

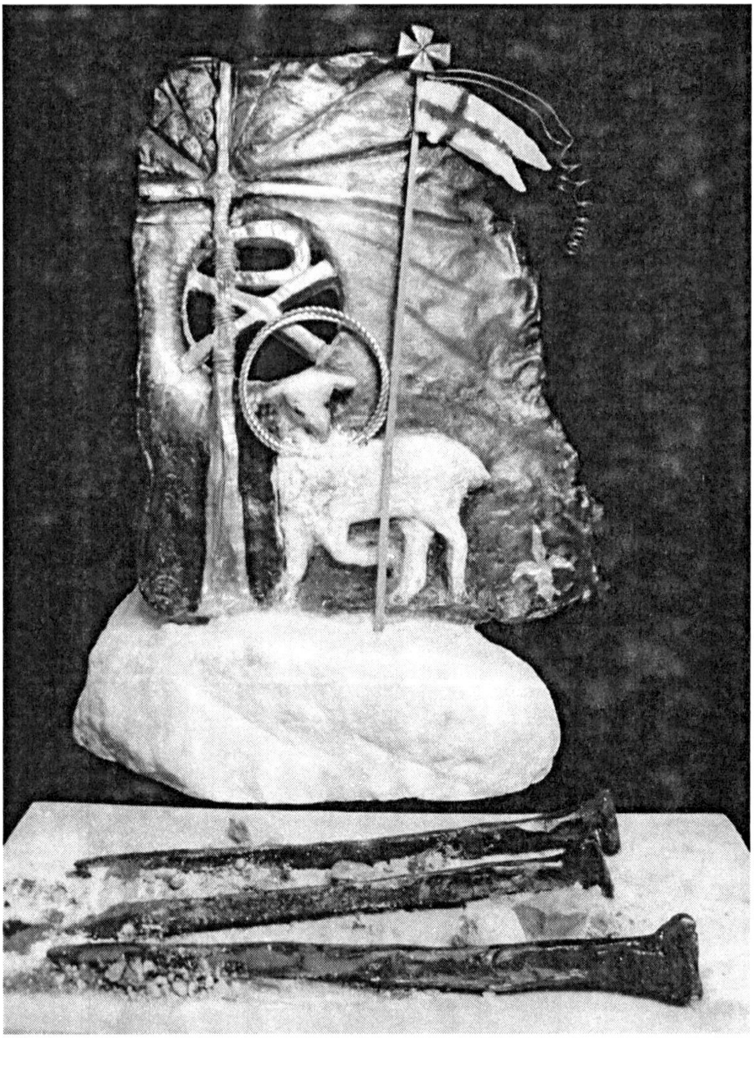

THE BLOOD OF THE LAMB

The Blood of the Lamb
Is shed freely for all
A sacrifice to the Father
In atonement

I Am the Lamb
I bleed freely for all
The first offering is made
In the dark recesses
Of the garden
The last when My side
Is opened by the lance

There is no one
To stay the hand
Of My betrayer
The catalyst to
My crucifixion
There is only
A heavenly messenger
Who brings Me comfort

There is no one
To stay the hand
Of my executioners
My Father will not
Interfere
He will not
Stop this crucifixion

I must do this alone
So from the Mount of Olives
To the Mount of Calvary
I bleed
A trail of blood and tears
A path
I call you to follow

Drop by drop
I give My
Life giving liquid
For you
It will wash you clean
Make your robes of scarlet
White as snow

I Am the Unblemished Lamb
The Perfect Holocaust
I Am silent before
The shearers
And upon the wooden altar
Of My cross
My life is offered
To the Father
And He accepts

Sin has a new master
You are free
Free at last
Come
Be washed
In the
Blood of the Lamb

Reflections

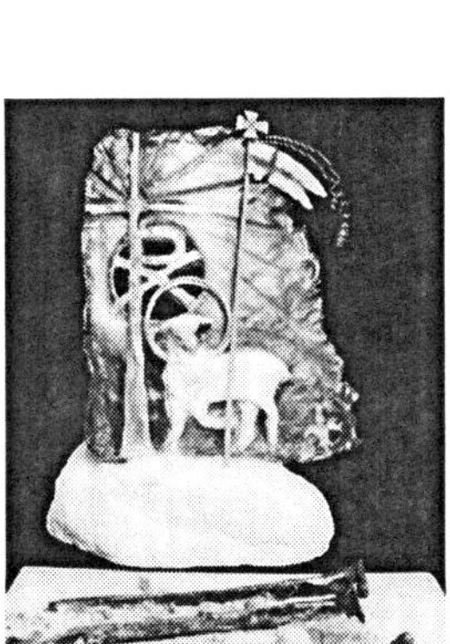

MY LOVE

My love
Is offered to all
Given freely
Presented to you
From Me

With My arms
Outstretched
Upon the cross

Yet there are some partakers

Who cannot accept this Truth

My Body and Blood
Are offered to all
Given freely
Presented to you
From Me

In the Bread and Wine
Of the Eucharist

Yet there are some partakers

Who cannot accept this Truth

I AM this Bread you eat

I AM this Wine you drink

I AM the Great I AM

I die for you

I live for you

Be a true partaker

Accept this wondrous gift

Eat and drink of Me

That I may nourish you

Body soul and spirit

Look upon the cross

Then look upon the altar

I AM here

Body—Blood—Soul—and Divinity

My love awaits you here

Reflections

FEELINGS

There is not a part of My body
That is not in torment
I ache
A deep indwelling
Slumbering continuous ache
Until some new trauma brings
The ache alive and it
Bursts into full-fledged agony

I have feelings

Pain is My constant companion
From the moment
Of My betrayal
There is anguish and heartbreak
And fear
Cold
Shivering raw fear

As I lay alone on the
Cold damp floor
I can taste the bile
In My mouth
As I drift
In and out of consciousness
After the scourging

The feeling of thorns
Digging and clawing
Their way into My skull
Through My hair
Matted with blood
Digging ever deeper
Inflicting pain from the
Orbs of My eyes to
Deep within My temples
And across My forehead

The plaited thorns are
Unyielding
As inward
They creep and seep
Causing My head to throb and
Pulsate with wave upon waves of pain
Even to move My face brings misery

I begin the walk and
My Body rebels against the effort

The feel of the hard-baked
Unyielding ground
As I fall
Time and again
My knees become battered
And bruised

The feeling of My clothes
Being torn from My Body
As I wait
And shiver in the breeze
All has been taken from Me
In poverty
I stand and I wait
I Am pushed down
Upon the cross

The feeling as
Nails are driven
The pounding reverberates
In My ears as
My hands and feet
Explode in pain

The feeling of
The roughness of the cross
On My torn and bloody back
As the cross is lifted up
And placed in the hole
In the ground

It drops with a thud
And I feel
My body erupt in terror
At the thought of falling and
Being ripped from the cross

But the nails hold fast

My hands and feet are being torn apart
And the slow agonizing process of
Dislocation of bone and sinew begins
I hang here
Waiting for death to come

The feeling of
Abandonment and fear
When I realize that
My earthly friends have
Deserted Me except for a loyal few
The feeling of helplessness
And Divine abandonment
When My Heavenly Father
Turns away
The feeling of death
As it wraps its arms about Me
As I surrender all to the Father
There is fear and trepidation
And resignation
And acceptance

And finally
The feeling of JOY
Floods My Being for
I know that My Father
Will approve of My sacrifice
And you
My people
Will find heaven
Open to receive you

Reflections

THE TORMENT

In torment
I suffer

The torment in My mind

Weakens Me

Tempts Me

Entices Me
To stop this pain
This suffering
This agony

After all
I Am God

I can put a stop

To this scenario

I can stop this brutality
Heaped upon Me

In a heartbeat
I can be
The Warrior King
The Jews
Are waiting for

The torment of My betrayal
Weighs heavy on My spirit
The kiss of a friend
Bruises My heart
More than My body

That My companion
Is capable of such
A heinous crime against Me
Is unthinkable
I come to save all
And he is lost and damned
And there is no way
I can stop him

The torment
When I look into My mother's eyes
She is in agony for Me
And this breaks My heart
We weep
She is strong and
Utters not a word
But the sadness in her eyes
Captures Me
She is crying
Her fiat—"**YES**"
To the Father once more
As she releases Me
Her only Son
To die

How can I do this
With a snap of My finger
A myriad of angels
Will rush to My rescue
And free Me
Wait
Stop
This is not the way

I Am He of whom
Prophets spoke
I Am The Lord God
I Am the Obedient Son
Meek and humble of heart
I must obey the Will of My Father

The torment in My mind
Is far greater than the
Battle in My tortured Body
With every step
I must choose
To go on
Knowing what awaits me
I must choose
To climb the hill
The place of My death
I must choose
To be nailed upon the cross
I must choose to die
This IS the Way
The only Way

I Am Victim and Priest
Upon this altar
Upon this cross
I offer Myself
In atonement
To the Father
For you
But in My humanity
I struggle
Just like you
But I do **not** fall

I must contend
Just like you
With the forces of evil
Waging war for My soul
And I will **NOT** fail

But little do they know
I Am salvation
For the masses
I Am the Way
I Am the Truth
I Am the Life

I AM That I AM
Look **TO** Me and
Learn **FROM** Me
Resist the torment
Be free

Reflections

HANDS PUSHING ME. HITTING ME.
ROUGH
UNYIELDING
SCRATCHING
ANGRY
BRUTAL
HATE

TOUCHES

Touches
The coldness
And hardness
Of the earth
As I kneel and pray
In agony

Touches
The kiss of My betrayer
Soft upon My cheek
Yet reeking of the agony
Yet to come

Touches
Rough unyielding hands
Tying Mine with rope and chains
Tight—Taut
Scratching—Bruising
My wrists—My neck
Jerking Me forward
With unnecessary violence
Angry hands
Pushing on Me
Hitting Me
As I stumble for
The chains upon
My feet

Touches
The stinging whip
Ripping My body apart

Touches
The thorns
Deeply piercing
Into My head

Touches
The softness of
Veronica's veil

Touches
The touch of
My mother's eyes
Softly weeping
As she looks upon My face

Touches
The touch of the cross
Upon My shoulder as I walk
Sapping My strength
Buckling My knees
Driving Me to the ground
The splinters of wood
Penetrating deeply
Imbedding themselves
In My tortured flesh

Touches
The feel of My Blood
As it runs down My face
To mingle with My tears
Dripping
Running down
My neck
My arms
My legs
Rivulets
Inching their way
Down
To the ground
Causing My footing
To become unsure

Touches
As I slip and
Fall to My knees
Again
And again
And again

Touches
The feel of My clothes
Sticking to Me
Held in place
By
My sweat
And My Blood

Touches
As My clothes
Are ripped and
Roughly torn
From
My body
Opening wounds
Removing skin

Touches
The cold iron nails
Hammered in
Ripping My hands
And feet asunder

Touches
The touch of a sponge
As it brushes My lips
With bitterness

Touches
The touch of death
As I give My Spirit
To My Father
And surrender
My Will to His

Reflections

I AM FORGIVENESS

I Am betrayed
I Am led away in chains
I Am condemned
And I forgive
I love

I Am scourged
I Am beaten
I Am crowned with thorns
Crucify Him
And I forgive
I love

I Am paraded
Through the streets
Like a criminal
A spectacle
For all to look upon
And scorn
I carry My cross
And I forgive
I love

I fall in weakness
In weariness
On My knees
I Am whipped
I walk the road
To My death alone
And I forgive
I love

I Am nailed to a cross
Raised in insolence
I Am derided mocked
All hail! King of the Jews!
And I forgive
I love

I bleed freely
I Am stripped of
All earthly possessions
I Am nothing
To the unbelieving
And everything
To the chosen
And I forgive
I love

I die
I Am buried
I rise
And I forgive
I love

Come all ye sinners
Come to the cross
Of your King
Don't stand back
Don't be afraid
I do not condemn you

I AM Forgiveness
I AM Love

Reflections

UNION WITH ME

Union with Me
Deep abiding
Union with Me

United to
My pain
My suffering
My death

Union with Me
As I walk the earth
Heal the sick
Raise the dead
Proclaim the Word

Union with Me
On My road of death
As I face
My judgment
Unfairly condemned

Union with Me
At My scourging
Whipped
Beaten
Disfigured

Union with Me
As you stand
With Me
To feel
The whip
As the whip master
Delivers blow
Upon blow
Upon blow

Union with Me
As My back is
On fire
And no water can
Quench its flame

Union with Me
As My head
Is pierced
With the thorns
Of iniquity

Union with Me
As I stand accused
And condemned
By the nation

The chosen of My Father

Union with Me
As Pilate hands Me over
As I walk
The road
Of death
Struggling with every step
With every breath
To remain alive
So I can die
A criminal's death

Union with Me
As I hang upon
The rugged cross
And shed My last
Drop of blood
For you

Union with Me
That you may know
The depth of My love

Union with Me
In life

In death

In glory

INRI

I GIVE ALL

I give all

I surrender

My life
My Blood
My Divinity
My humanity

The enormity of it
Is beyond
All comprehension

I bleed for you

I suffer

Untold sufferings
Beyond all imagination

I endure so much
And would again
For My beloved
My creation

I give all

My Body to the blows
Inflicted upon it
My will to the Father
That His will
Not Mine be done

My heart to torment
That you may be free
My mind to acceptance
Of the fate
I was born to fulfill

I give all
My Blood
Its significance
Is still overlooked
By many

My sweat
Even this
Is liquid refreshment
For parched souls

My tears
Shed in bitterness
And pain
That you may come
In rejoicing

I give all

A crumpled man
Broken and bruised
Hanging on a cross
A laughing stock
A curse
The epitome
Of defeat
Yet
I Am Life
And My victory
Is beyond measure
I will reign eternal

I give all
I AM risen
I sit in glory
At the right hand
Of the Father
We are One

I give all
That you may
Follow Me
That you may endure
In the face of
Hardships
Loneliness
Suffering and pain

I give all

That you may come
Unto Me
And dwell with Me
In My Father's House

I give all

Because you are not able
To appease the Father
I do this willingly
For you
I hold nothing back
I give all
Let My love
Engulf you

Look upon the cross
And see that love
Manifested in agony
And projected in joy

I give all

I give all
To the Father
For you
Receive My gift
And give
Your all
To Me

Reflections

HUMILITY

Humility
Born out of humiliation
Degradation
Agony
Pain
And
Death

I Am meek
And humble of heart
I Am strength
The mighty arm of the Father

I Am sinfulness
Vile and ugly
A stigma
I Am dejected
By My Father

And this burden
I willingly carry

I Am contradiction
A symbol of life
An enigma to some
A puzzle to most
Salvation to the chosen

I Am degraded
Spit upon
This oral discharge
Usually finds a place
In filth
I become that filth

I Am agony
Gut-retching pain
Tears at
My very soul
My body trembles
I literally bounce
Upon that dirty
Naked floor
I shake and
My teeth chatter
I am cold
So cold
And there is nothing
That can warm Me
Constant badgering
And no one to bring Me
Comfort as I await My fate

I Am humiliated
Before the crowd
My clothes are torn away
I lose all
Even My garments
At the hands of angry men

I Am poor
And humble of heart
I Am derided
And cursed
And mocked
They laugh in My face
They demand a sign
Come down off that cross
Not this day
The King of glory
Is hidden in the
Flesh of humanity

I Am humility
I give you witness
I Am love
I Am mercy
I Am forgiveness
Come follow Me

I lower Myself
To become
One of My creatures
I walk among you
My Divinity concealed
The Great I AM
Pure Spirit
The Omnipotent God
Leaves heaven and
Comes down to earth
I AM one of you
And you know Me not

I CRY

I cry
From a sadness of heart
For lost generations
Who will not change
Their ways
I cry

I cry
For you
I—the Lord of Lord
And King of Kings
The Creator of all things
I cry

I cry
In surrender
For the pain
I will endure
For the aloneness
In that cold dark garden
For the desertion of friends
I cry

I cry
In agony
From the stripes
Upon My back
From the crown
Upon My head

From the nails
That pierce My
Hands and feet
I cry

I cry out
As I hang
Upon the cross
Surrendering all
To the will of My Father
Our Father
I cry

I cry
In My humanity
I cry
For I Am scorned
And ridiculed
And beaten
And murdered
I bear all in silence
I endure all the pain
For you
For your salvation
I cry

I cry
The tears of your Master
Free you forever
My sacrifice
Opens the gates of heaven
And eternity
I cry

Reflections

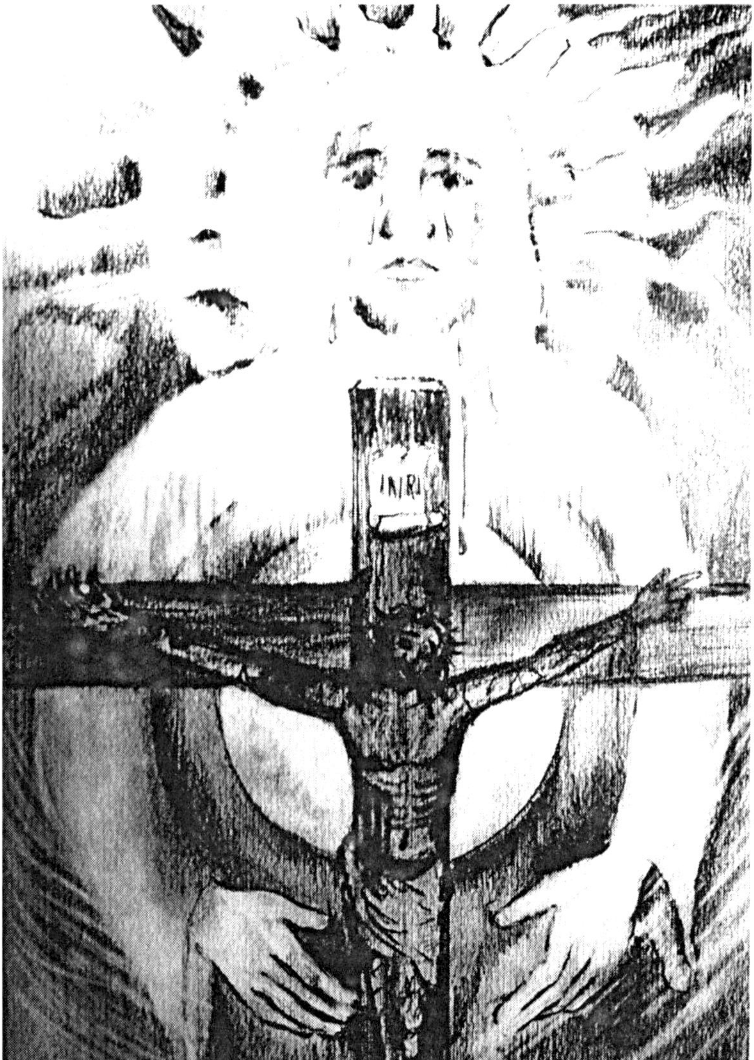
INRI

AND THE FATHER CRIES

As I pray in the garden
And beg for His will
He knows My destiny
And speaks not a word
He sends one of His angels
To minister to Me
He looks at His Son
And the Father cries

The Father looks down
From above
As I Am betrayed and
Chained
That cold dark night
And the Father cries

He watches as I Am
Condemned by His chosen
Brought before the tribunal
Of the just
Unjustly accused
He watches from on high
And the Father cries

As I Am scourged
And degraded
Abused and bruised
He silently watches
His heart breaking
Knowing He cannot interfere
And the Father cries

He listens with heavy heart
To the condemnation of the masses
The words branded in His mind
Crucify Him   Crucify Him
The innocent becomes guilt
The sinless becomes sin
And the cross becomes
The salvation of man
And the Father cries

As I stumble and fall
On My way to Calvary
No hand can He offer
As My body is pierced
He closes His eyes in misery
And the Father cries

As I hang in agony
Searching for His will
Crying out for His presence
The Father turns away
And the Father cries

I surrender My spirit
Give My all for Him
And for you
And the Father is pleased
Joy fills His Being
For He knows that
Heaven's gates are open
And the Father cries

Reflections

THE SORROWFUL MYSTERIES

THE AGONY IN THE GARDEN

Imagine a Father and a Son

Imagine a profound love between them
Formed before
The beginning of time
Nurtured in infinity

Imagine them separated

Their close contact now severed
No conversation
No touch
Unreachable —
Unthinkable

This is the beginning
Of My Agony
This is what brings Me
To My knees

As the sins of the world
Are laid upon My shoulders
This is what I experience
As I lay prostrate
On the ground in the Garden

Unquenchable agony
Floods My being

I bleed

My friends lie sleeping

And I suffer alone

A deep ache
Unspeakable torment

Oh Take it away, Father
Take this cup from Me

Inexplicitly,
A peace fills Me

From deep within
I find comfort

Oh, Father, I love you so
I accept My destiny
A decision made before Creation

Only, Father, I didn't know
It would hurt so much

I AM alone

THE SCOURGING AT THE PILLAR

The physical abuse
Heaped upon My body
Is beyond the depth
Of any pain
I have experienced

But what truly troubles Me

Brings Me to tears

Is the fact that I have
No one

No one to turn to

No one to run to

To hold Me
To kiss away the pain

No shoulder I can cry on

Or arms to enfold Me

No one to comfort Me

I AM alone

THE CROWNING WITH THORNS

My princely crown
Is replaced
By a crown of mockery
A crown that inflicts
Wounds upon My royal head

There is no heavenly throne
To sit upon
Only a cold marble floor

My subjects do not honor Me
Instead I Am ridiculed
And beaten
And laughed at
I Am a buffoon in their eyes
They look
But they do not see
Their Redeemer
Whom they abuse
There is no love or compassion
In them

I bear the brunt of their cruelty
No one is here to buffet their blows
To silence their words

I AM alone

THE CARRYING OF THE CROSS

I walk alone

The cross upon My back

Until Simon of Cyrene

Is forced to help Me

He is not willing

He is not My friend

He balks at the order

But he is pressed
Into My service

How do you come to Me

How do you carry your cross

Willingly

Or must you also be
Pressed into My service

I AM alone

THE CRUCIFIXION

In misery
In agony
I Am crucified

There are none who can
Comfort Me or
Take away My pain

My mother and My beloved
Are here
There is nothing
They can do for Me
We weep together

My Father,
My Father,
Why have You abandoned Me
I want to reach out
And touch Him

I AM alone

I close My eyes in death
In perfect surrender
Oh, Father
You are here
Hold Me
I AM **NOT** alone
I was **NEVER ALONE**

Reflections

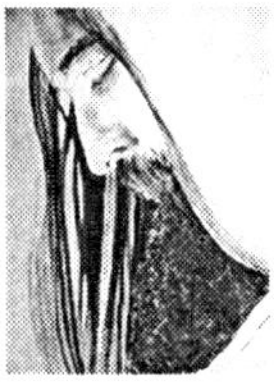

SWEET BLOOD, BROKEN BODY

My Body is broken
Torn asunder
Sweet Blood
Sweet purifying liquid
Like dew from heaven
It is shed for you
For all mankind
Slowly dripping
Drop by precious drop
From innumerable wounds
Inflicted upon
This Holy Body
Sweet Blood
It flows like a river
Come
Be washed
In the Blood
Of the Lamb

My Body is broken
Offered to the Father
As Bread upon the altar
My Blood is shed
Offered to the Father
As Wine upon the altar
At the hands of My priests
In your church
Come
Partake
Sweet honey to your lips

Dripping from My dying Body
Given in love and sacrifice
Taste and see the goodness
Of the Lord

I Am wretched and alone
As I hang here
Bleeding
Receive Me
In Body and in Blood

Take Me in and know
That I AM God
And this is sweet
Refreshment for your
Weary soul

Sweet sacrament
Come
Eat of My Flesh and
Drink of My Sweet Blood
Come to the everlasting banquet
Your salvation
My death
Come
Eat
Drink
Be healed

Be saved

Reflections

THE BATTLE

This is the battle
I was born to fight
For the souls of the righteous

This is the battle
I was born to win

I do not battle
Against the Romans
But against
The forces of evil

I AM
The Heavenly Warrior King
Battered
Bruised
Defiled
So that you may be made
Whole and clean

I AM
The King of Kings
And yet

I endure
The chastisement of men

I endure
The feeling of
Wretchedness

I endure
The pain and agony

I endure
The abandonment of friends

I endure
The abandonment of My Father

I endure
The coldness of death

So that you may have life
Eternally
With the Father and Me

This Battle is won this today

Reflections

THE LIGHT

There is light
Emanating from
My bruised heart
The Bread of Life

Let this light
Shine in you
And through you
So that others may
See Me
In you

This heart broken
In anguish and pain
In torment and anxiety
Pierced with a lance
Beats for you
Lives for you
Nourishes you

This Body
Broken bruised bloodied
And tortured for you
Sheds Its Blood for you
In agony—in pain
In sorrow
Its wretchedness
Proclaimed among the masses
And willingly
Given to the Father

Yet I rise
Glorified
Perfected in Love
Commissioned by the Father
To be the Savior of the world

I Am no longer alone
No longer abandoned
No longer suffering
I Am embraced by the Father
Praised by the choirs
Of heavenly hosts
Worshipped by the saints

This cross
This symbol of death
And infamy
Becomes the means
To the end
End to this earthly life
And
The beginning of your eternity

My Body and My Blood
Become the Bread of Life
The Cup of Eternal Salvation
Come to My banquet
Prepared for you
With these pierced hands
And heart

Receive Me
Eat
Drink
And become
The Body of Christ

This Eucharist
This is the Great I AM
The Christ
This is the Great I AM
Here before you

Where is the adoration
Where is the wonder
Where is the reverence

My anguish is renewed
My agony revisited
When you look upon Me
Your God
So lightly
Without devotion
Without love

I Am hurt once more
I Am brought down
To My knees

The sins I carry are these

I Am awash in tears once more
I cry for you

Dry My tears with your fervor
Bring joy to My heart once more
For I bring the greatest of gifts
To you

At the Banquet of Life

I bring My Love

Receive Me

Your God
In awe
In worship
In adoration

Become

My light
Unto the world

Become

THE BODY OF CHRIST

Reflections

"**It is finished!** What are your final thoughts? You have walked with Him; you have looked *Through His Eyes.* May you come to realize how much He suffered—so great was His love for you. May He bless you and keep you in the palm of His nail-scarred hands."

Anna

ILLUSTRATOR'S PAGES

As you turn these pages, you will find additional images by the illustrator, Regina-Champagne Babin

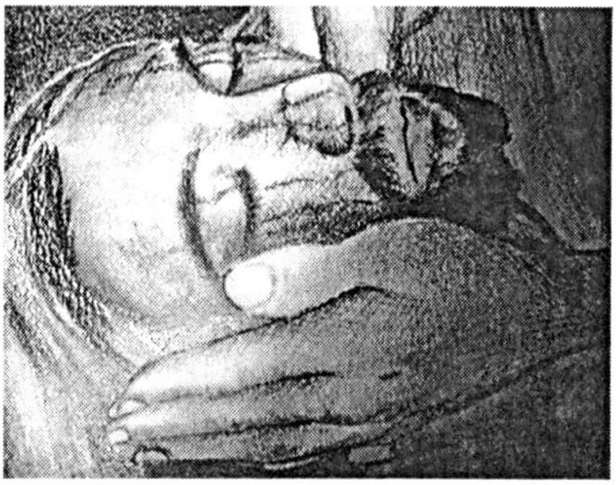
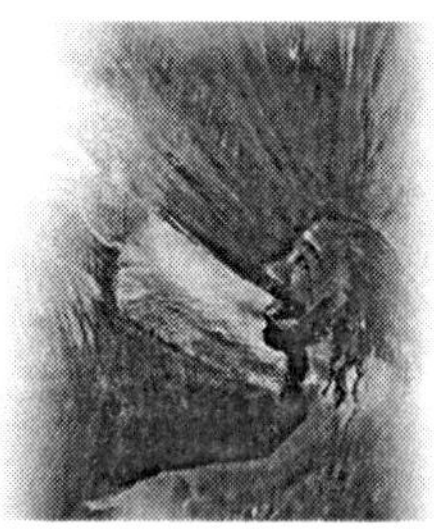
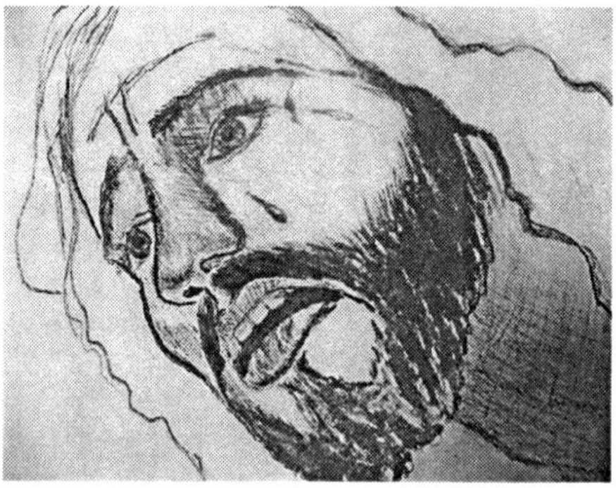

Couer de mon Couer

Included here is
an original lead sheet.

This song was composed by
Regina-Champagne Babin,
the illustrator

Heart of my Heart : COEUR DE MON COEUR
LEAD SHEET
Moderato
Heart of my heart. Vi-sion of my sight. Soul of my e-ter-nal
li-ving soul, you've made pure love songs true.
When I look in-to your eyes, I'm o-bli-vi-ous to this world
I can feel e-ter-ni-ty. You live passionately with-in me.
You've been a Love Song from the start. You are the
rhythm of my heart, You are the melody of my soul.
FRANCAIS
You have made my life whole. COEUR DE MON COEUR,
VISION DE MA VUE, ÂME DE MON ÂME VIVANTE ÉTERNELLE.
VOUS AVEZ FAIT TOUTES LES CHANSONS D'AMOUR VENIR VRAI.
QUAND JE REGARDE DON VOS YEUX.
JE SUIS INCONSCIENT À CE MONDE. JE PUIS VOIR L'ÉTERNITÉ.
VOUS ÊTES PATIONATELY CHEZ MOI.

Notes / Reflections

Notes / Reflections

Notes / Reflections

Notes / Reflections

Priscilla Freeman, the spiritual author of Through His Eyes, went to be with the Lord on October 3rd, 2013. She was unable to be here to see the first publication of her book. She had a slow illness but the Joy of the Lord was her strength. "Couer de mon Couer, Heart pf My Heart" has been changed to "Priscilla's Song."

"Couer de mon Couer, Heart of my Heart"

"Priscilla's Song"

Draft 1

Music and Lyrics by
Regina - Champagne Babin
Scored by Logan Boudreaux

Liturgical

10
eyes, I'm o - bli-vi -ous to this world. I can feel e-ter-ni - ty.
eyes, I'm o - bli-vi -ous to this world. I can feel e-ter-ni - ty.
eyes, I'm o - bli-vi -ous to this world. I can feel e-ter-ni - ty.
eyes, I'm o - bli-vi -ous to this world. I can feel e-ter-ni - ty.

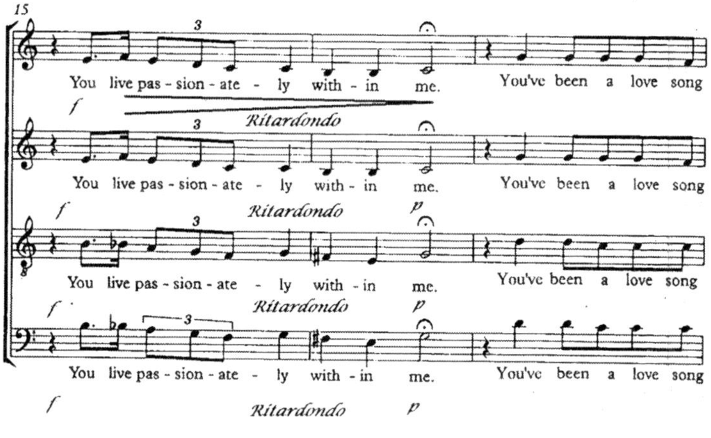
15
You live pas - sion - ate - ly with - in me. You've been a love song
f
Ritardondo
You live pas - sion - ate - ly with - in me. You've been a love song
f
Ritardondo
p
You live pas - sion - ate - ly with - in me. You've been a love song
f
Ritardondo
p
You live pas - sion - ate - ly with - in me. You've been a love song
f
Ritardondo
p

18
from the start. You are the rhy-thm of my heart. You
from the start. You are the rhy-thm of my heart. You
from the start. You are the rhy-thm of my heart. You
from the start. You are the rhy-thm of my heart. You

22
3
are the me-lo - dy of my soul. You have made my life whole. Coeur de mon
Emotional mf p mf
are the me-lo - dy of my soul. You have made my life whole. Coeur de mon
Emotional mf p mf
are the me lo - dy of my soul. You have made my life whole. Coeur de mon
Emotional mf p mf
are the me-lo - dy of my soul. You have made my life whole. Coeur de mon
Emotional mf p mf

27
Coeur, vi-si-on de ma vue, ame de mon ame vi vante e-ter-nelle.
Coeur, vi-si-on de ma vue, ame de mon ame vi vante e-ter-nelle.
Coeur, vi-si-on de ma vue, ame de mon ame vi vante e-ter-nelle.
Coeur, vi-si-on de ma vue, ame de mon ame vi vante e-ter-nelle.

32
vous a - vez fait toutes les chan - sons d' amour ve - nir vrai.
mf p
vous a - vez fait toutes les chan - sons d' amour ve - nir vrai.
mf p
vous a - vez fait toutes les chan - sons d' amour ve - nir vrai.
mf p
vous a - vez fait toutes les chan - sons d' amour ve - nir vrai.
mf p

35
Quand je re- gar - de don vos yeux. Je suis in-con-scient a ce
Quand je re- gar - de don vos yeux. Je suis in-con-scient a ce
Quand je re- gar - de don vos yeux. Je suis in-con-scient a ce
Quand je re- gar - de don vos yeux. Je suis in-con-scient a ce
38
monde. Je puis voir L' e - ter - nite.
Ritardondo
With great emotion to the end
ppp
fade away
monde. Je puis voir L' e - ter - nite.
Ritardondo
With great emotion to the end
ppp
fade away
monde. Je puis voir L' e - ter - nite.
Retardondo
With great emotion to the end
ppp
fade away
monde. Je puis voir L' e - ter - nite.
Retardondo
With great emotion to the end
ppp
fade away

Reflections

Reflections

Reflections

Reflections

CPSIA information can be obtained
at www.ICGtesting.com
Printed in the USA
FFOW05n2211071014

9 780741 467768